Drama for Students, Volume 18

Project Editor: David Galens

Editorial: Anne Marie Hacht, Michelle Kazensky, Ira Mark Milne, Pam Revitzer, Kathy Sauer, Timothy J. Sisler, Jennifer Smith, Carol Ullmann

Research: Michelle Campbell, Tracie Richardson

Permissions: Debra J. Freitas

Manufacturing: Stacy Melson

Imaging and Multimedia: Leitha Etheridge-Sims, Lezlie Light, Dave G. Oblender, Kelly A. Quin, Luke Rademacher

Product Design: Pamela A. E. Galbreath

© 2003 by Gale. Gale is an imprint of Gale, Inc., a division of Cengage Learning Inc.

Gale and Design® and Cengage Learning™ are trademarks used herein under license.

For more information, contact

Gale
27500 Drake Rd.
Farmington Hills, MI 48331-3535
Or you can visit our Internet site at http://www.gale.com

ALL RIGHTS RESERVED
No part of this work covered by the copyright hereon may be reproduced or used in any form or by any means—graphic, electronic, or mechanical, including photocopying, recording, taping, Web distribution, or information storage retrieval systems—without the written permission of the publisher.

For permission to use material from this product, submit your request via Web at http://www.gale-edit.com/permissions, or you may download our Permissions Request form and submit your request by fax or mail to:

Permissions Department
Gale, Inc.
27500 Drake Rd.
Farmington Hills, MI 48331-3535
Permissions Hotline: 248-699-8006 or 800-877-4253, ext. 8006
Fax: 248-699-8074 or 800-762-4058

Since this page cannot legibly accommodate all copyright notices, the acknowledgments constitute an extension of the copyright notice.

While every effort has been made to ensure the reliability of the information presented in this publication, The Gale Group, Inc. does not guarantee the accuracy of the data contained herein. The Gale Group, Inc. accepts no payment for listing; and inclusion in the publication of any organization, agency, institution, publication, service, or individual does not imply endorsement of the editors or publisher. Errors brought to the attention of the publisher and verified to the satisfaction of the publisher will be corrected in future editions.

ISBN 0-7876-6815-X
ISSN 1094-9232

Printed in the United States of America
10 9 8 7 6 5 4 3 2 1

Endgame

Samuel Beckett

1957

Introduction

Endgame is Samuel Beckett's second published play. The plot is continuous, unbroken by separate scenes or acts. Roger Blin first produced this play in France at the Royal Court, in 1957, and later Blin and Georges Devine produced it again in an English production. Both were badly received by almost all London critics. Only after the now famous Paris production of 1964, starring Patrick Magee and Jack Macgowran in the roles of Hamm and Clov, was

Endgame recognized as a masterpiece.

As the play opens, Hamm is dying in a world that seems to be coming to an end. Hamm takes satisfaction in knowing that all of existence may fade to nothing. Hamm is confined to a chair, and throughout the play he discards, reluctantly, the continuing prospects of life: food; painkillers; his servant Clov, on whom he is totally dependent; the pole that enables him to move his wheelchair; and holding the dog, on which he lavishes his affection.

Hamm's parents, Nagg and Nell, having lost their legs many years ago in a bicycle accident, live in ashbins from which they occasionally emerge only to be cursed by their son. His mother dies and Hamm, knowing that Clov is leaving him, prepares for his last battle, first to outlive his father and then to face inevitable death without the help of the few objects that have given him comfort in his final days. Hamm soliloquizes in terms of the last moves in chess, a king evading checkmate as long as possible with stern asides on religion, "Get out of here and love one another! Lick your neighbor as yourself!" He echoes Pozzo's gravedigger aphorism in *Waiting for Godot* when he says, "The end is in the beginning and yet you go on." Clov prepares to leave, hating Hamm for past wrongs, yet now without pity for Hamm.

Author Biography

Samuel Barclay Beckett was born in Foxrock County, Dublin, Ireland, on April 13, 1906. He was the second of two sons of a Protestant Anglo-Irish couple. As a young boy, he was quite energetic and excelled at sports such as cricket, tennis, and boxing. He studied at Earlsfort House in Dublin and then at Portora Royal School in Enniskillen, the same school Oscar Wilde had attended. It was here that he first began to learn French, one of the two languages in which he would write.

He received a degree in romance languages from Trinity College, Dublin. He taught in Belfast before going to Paris as *lecteur d'anglais* at the École Normale Supérieure; there, in 1928, he met fellow Dubliner James Joyce, with whom he formed a lasting friendship. Beckett was one of Joyce's assistants in the construction of *Work in Progress,* later titled *Finnegan's Wake.* Inspired by the Parisian literary scene, Beckett began writing. His first published writing was an essay on Joyce (1929). His first story, "Assumption," appeared in *Transition* in 1929, and in 1930 he returned as lecturer to Trinity College, Dublin.

In 1930, Beckett published his first poem, "Whoroscope." Shortly thereafter, he published a study of the recently deceased Proust, an author Beckett admired tremendously. Beckett quickly realized the academic life was not for him and left

Trinity College to become a full-time writer. He then embarked on five unsettled, solitary years in Germany, France, Ireland, and London before settling permanently in France in 1937. A collection of stories, *More Pricks than Kicks* (1934) was followed by a number of full-length novels, including the comic novel *Murphy* (1938) and *Watt* (1953), both written in English.

Walking home late one night with friends, Beckett was stabbed and nearly killed. Recuperating, Beckett received attention from a French acquaintance, Suzanne Deschevaux-Dusmesnil, who would become his life companion and wife, though they would not marry until 1961. Beckett and Suzanne worked for the French Resistance, narrowly escaped the Gestapo, and then moved to unoccupied France, where Beckett worked on a farm in exchange for room and board and wrote his novel *Watt*.

Many consider the beginning of his writing in French (1947–1950) his most prolific creative period. Beckett's trilogy—*Molloy* (1951), *Mallone Dies* (1951), and *The Unnamable* (1953)—were all originally written in French and all three are interior monologues or soliloquies. His first French novel, *Mercier et Camier*, predicts the form of *Waiting for Godot*, with its wandering duo, minimalist style and repetition, but was not published until years later. Also in 1947, he wrote his first play, *Eleutheria*, which he would not allow to be published during his lifetime and which, after his death, became a cause of great controversy when Beckett's American publisher, Barney Rosset, released an English translation against the wishes of the Beckett estate. In 1948–1949, Beckett wrote *En attendant Godot* or *Waiting for Godot*. Beckett's highly distinctive, despairing, yet curiously exhilarating voice reached a wide audience and won public acclaim with the Paris performance in 1953 of *En attendant Godot*. Beckett became widely known as a playwright associated with the theater of the absurd, whose use of the stage and of dramatic narrative and symbolism revolutionized drama in England and deeply influenced later playwrights.

In the 1950s and 1960s, Beckett's playwriting continued with a series of masterworks including *Endgame*, *Krapp's Last Tape*, and *Happy Days*. He wrote his first radio plays and created innovative prose fiction, including *How It Is* (1961) and *The Lost Ones* (1970).

In the 1970s, Beckett continued to interest himself in the productions of his plays, wrote television plays for the BBC, and began the autobiographical novel *Company*. In the 1980s, he crafted more prose works (*Ill Seen Ill Said* and *Westward Ho*) and more plays (including *Rockaby* and *Ohio Impromptu*). His last major work was *Stirrings Still* (1986).

In 1986, Beckett began to suffer from emphysema. After his first hospitalization, he wrote in bed, producing his final work, the poem "What is the Word." After moving into the nursing home Le Tiers Temps, Beckett's deteriorating health prevented him from new writing, but he continued to translate previous works. Suzanne died on July 17, 1989, and Beckett died on December 22 of the same year. He is buried in Montparnasse Cemetery in Paris.

Beckett was awarded the Nobel Prize for literature in 1969 but did not attend the presentation ceremony.

Plot Summary

The play opens by establishing the only *mise-enscéne* of the play. Clov begins his daily ritual of drawing back the curtains of two windows (first the sea window and then the earth window). He uncovers two ashbins and then Hamm, who is still asleep. Clov delivers the play's opening soliloquy, setting up the thematic tension between characters that seek an ending, either to life or their habitual lifestyles, and their impotency in activating the means to that end. Clov states, "I can't be punished anymore," which reinforces his discontent as Hamm's servant and expresses his desire to leave Hamm altogether.

Hamm delivers his first soliloquy and we are introduced to the master-servant relationship between Hamm and Clov. Hamm addresses his bloodstained handkerchief as "Old Stancher" and is convinced that his suffering is greater than all others and establishes the dual metaphor throughout the play: the rhetoric of chess strategy and drama as game and competition. The play's dialogue begins with the word "finished" and Hamm expresses his wish to begin the day by going to bed. Hamm is terrified of being left alone and will do anything to keep Clov with him. Hamm asks Clov for his painkiller and Clov denies him. This is the first of six times that Hamm will ask Clov for his painkiller throughout the play. Later, when Hamm asks Clov why he does not kill him, Clov tells him that it is because he does not know the combination of the cupboard where the food supply is stored. Hamm dismisses Clov to the kitchen and then chastises his father, Nagg, who has emerged from one of the ashbins, demanding food. Hamm whistles Clov in to feed Nagg, and then Hamm orders Clov to push Nagg back into the bin and close the lid. Hamm continues to try to draw Clov into conversation but fails.

Nell, Hamm's mother, is now introduced. Both she and Nagg, the two elderly characters of the play, are in ashbins, and although they are confined to these ashbins, they still strive for love and romance:

> NELL: What is it, my pet? (Pause.) Time for love?
>
> NAGG: Were you asleep?
>
> NELL: Oh, no!
>
> NAGG: Kiss me!
>
> NELL: We can't.
>
> NAGG: Try. (Their heads strain towards each other, fail to meet, fall apart again.)
>
> NELL: Why this farce, day after day?

Nagg and Nell discuss their loss of sight, hearing, and teeth, raging against Hamm for not providing them with adequate food and a regular change of sawdust in their ashbins. They tell each other jokes and reminisce over their romantic youth.

One of the jokes Nagg tells is of an old Jewish tailor who took more than three months to make a decent pair of trousers, the results of which were more satisfactory than God's six-day effort to create the world.

Hamm, annoyed by their nostalgia, interrupts his parents to tell them that he is experiencing physical distress. Nagg chuckles at Hamm's pain. Nell concedes that "nothing is truly funnier than unhappiness." Hamm demands silence and pleads for an end to his torment: "Will this never finish?" Nagg disappears into the ashbin, but Nell remains. Hamm shouts, "My kingdom for a nightman!" (a play on Shakespeare's *Richard III's* "My kingdom for a horse!" speech) and beckons Clov to rid him of Nagg and Nell.

Next is extended dialogue between Hamm and Clov. Hamm demonstrates that he is the center of attention. Clov again refuses Hamm his painkiller (for the third time), and Hamm demands that Clov take him for a spin around the room in his armchair, after which he ends up in the exact center of the room. While on the tour, Hamm lays his hand against the wall and says, "Beyond is the ... other hell."

Hamm tells Clov to observe the weather conditions outside through the earth window and the sea widow via the telescope. What follows could be out of a Charlie Chaplin movie for Beckett inserts slapstick antics in Clov's confusion about getting the ladder or the telescope first. Hamm demands the weather report, and Clov, moving about with the ladder and telescope at Hamm's command, is eventually able to inform him that both the earth and sea windows are "corpsed." This insight confirms Hamm's worst fears that nothing exists outside their shelter. For Hamm, there is nothing in the world, and the only conclusion is death and extinction.

Hamm continues to interrogate Clov, who tries to change the discussion by announcing that he has found a flea in his trousers. This sign of life upsets Hamm, who directs Clov, "But humanity might start from there all over again! Catch him, for the love of God!" Clov continues in a Chaplin-like scenario, trying to rid himself of the flea before they continue:

> HAMM: Did you get him?
>
> CLOV: Looks like it. (He drops the tin and adjusts his trousers.) Unless he's laying doggo.
>
> HAMM: Laying! Lying you mean. Unless he's lying doggo…. Use your head, can't you. If he was laying we'd be [b——]ed.

While bleak, Beckett combines the elements of tragedy and comedy flawlessly. Hamm and Clov discuss their possibilities of escape from their situation. They discuss the possibility of using a raft to go south through what may be shark-infested waters. Hamm asks Clov for his painkiller for the fourth time, and Clov refuses once again. Hamm tells Clov, "One day you'll be blind, like me. You'll be sitting there, a speck in the void, forever, like me.... Yes, one day you'll know what it is, you'll be like me, except that you won't have had pity on anyone and because there won't be anyone left to pity you." Hamm hopes to discourage Clov's leaving and reminds him that he took him in when he was a child and took care of him as a father would take care of his own child. While that may be true, Clov again threatens to leave. Hamm asks Clov to fetch him the toy dog that Clov has been making.

Clov brings out the toy dog, which has only three legs. Like the characters of the play, the toy dog is also crippled. Hamm happily takes the dog. This portion is dominated by discussion of what "goes on in the end."

The next section develops Clov's rebellion against Hamm. Hamm demands his gaff but is unable to move without Clov's assistance. Hamm tells a story of a mad painter who, believing the end of the world had come, was assigned to an insane asylum. Hamm would visit him and lead him to the window to show him the bountiful world outside, but the painter would retreat to his corner because "all he had seen was ashes."

Questioned by Hamm whether or not "this thing has gone on long enough," Clov agrees that it has, and while Hamm is stuck, Clov can leave Hamm. Hamm asks for a good-bye kiss, but Clov refuses. Hamm asks how he will know whether or not Clov has left or died in his kitchen, since the stench of rotting corpses is throughout the place.

Clov's answer is to set the alarm clock: if it rings he has gone, if it does not he is dead. Clov sets the alarm clock up and it rings:

CLOV: The end is terrific!

HAMM: I prefer the middle.

Hamm, for the fifth time, requests his painkiller and again Clov denies him. Hamm asks Clov to wake up Nagg. Hamm promises Nagg a sugarplum if he will listen to a story Hamm would like to tell. Nagg agrees. Next is a long monologue by Hamm. Hamm recalls a poor man and his baby who on Christmas Eve had once sought Hamm's kindness. Hamm tells the story with zeal, remembering his eventual agreement to take the man into his service and provide for his son. It becomes clear that the story Hamm is telling is that of Clov's father and how Clov came to be with Hamm. Hamm relishes his power over the others.

Hamm prays to God for salvation. Hamm orders both Clov and Nagg to pray to God, but Hamm cries in agony, "The bastard! He doesn't exist!" Nagg curses Hamm: "Yes, I hope I'll live till then, to hear you calling me like when you were a tiny boy, and were frightened, in the dark, and I was your only hope." Nagg, unable to get Nell to respond to his knocks on her ashbin lid, goes back into his ashbin and closes the lid.

Hamm continues to tell his story. Hamm sends Clov to see if Nell is dead. Clov replies, "Looks like it." Hamm asks Clov to check and see if Nagg is dead. Clov raises Nagg's ashbin lid and says,

"Doesn't look like it." Hamm asks what he is doing, and Clov replies, "He's crying," to which Hamm says, "Then he's living."

Hamm goes again for a spin around the room. Again, there is no light from the earth, and the sea is calm. Hamm accepts the world's condition and asks for his father but receives no response. Clov is sent to see if Nagg has heard either of Hamm's two calls. Clov reports that Nagg has heard only one call but is not certain if it was Hamm's first or second call.

Hamm asks for a lap rug, which Clov does not provide. Clov refuses to show Hamm any affection when Hamm asks for a kiss. Hamm asks for his toy dog but then changes his mind. Clov goes to the kitchen to kill the rat he has discovered there before it dies.

Hamm's next monologue begins calmly and nostalgically and builds feelings of guilt as well as curiosity about what happens after the end of the play.

> HAMM: There I'll be, in the old shelter, alone against my silence and … (he hesitates) … the stillness. If I can hold my peace, and sit quiet, it will be all over with sound, motion, all over and done with.

Clov was unable to kill the rat in the kitchen and the time for Hamm's painkiller has finally arrived. Clov now tells Hamm, after all of his requests, that the supply has been depleted. Clov seriously considers leaving Hamm. Hamm tells

Clov to look at the world outside "Since it's calling you."

Clov delivers his final monologue and realizes that he must learn to suffer. He and Hamm debate the state of the outside world and Hamm protests that he does not care what has happened. Clov reminds Hamm that he refused to provide Mother Pegg oil for her lamp and continues to tell Hamm harshly that Mother Pegg died of darkness. And so we believe that Mother Pegg's death was in part due to Hamm.

Hamm asks for the toy dog and Clov hits him on the head with it. Hamm pleads that Clov use an axe or gaff. When Clov announces that there are no more coffins, Hamm says, "Then let it end!" Hamm and Clov end their relationship and agree to go their separate ways.

Hamm's final monologue begins, "Old endgame lost of old, play and lose and have done with losing." Clov, dressed for his departure, enters and watches Hamm. After his monologue, Hamm calls twice for his father. There is no answer. Hamm then throws away the toy dog and his whistle and calls for Clov, who does not respond. Hamm covers his face with "Old Stancher," the bloodstained handkerchief. Hamm, blind and paralyzed, seems to have chosen against life. Clov, standing in his travel clothes, is confronted with the choice to remain or walk out and live in an unknown world. Whether this will work out or not, Clov does not know nor does the audience.

Characters

Clov

Clov is Hamm's servant, and he follows his master's wishes, despite being treated horribly. Crippled but not incapacitated, Clov is capable of leaving the shelter he has known his entire life and of taking his chances in the "other hell" beyond the walls. Clov shows that he is capable of handling tasks and life, and at the end of the play he prepares to leave Hamm and take his chances in the outside world.

Hamm

Hamm is dying in a world that seems to be ending. Hamm is blind and confined to a wheelchair. He is selfish and wants always to be the center of attention and considers himself something of a god-like character. He berates his servant Clov, upon whom he is completely dependent. His parents, Nagg and Nell, live in ashbins and occasionally emerge only to be berated by their son. Though the world may be coming to an end, Hamm takes satisfaction in knowing that perhaps all existence may fade to extinction. He hopes to exist long enough only to outlive his father.

Nagg

Nagg is Hamm's father. He and his wife now live in ashbins, having lost their legs in a bicycling accident years ago. Although their current situation is bleak, there are moments in the play where we understand that in their youth, Nagg and Nell had a great and wondrous love. They still reach for that love, despite the horrid conditions and their ungrateful son.

Nell

Nell is Hamm's mother. She, like Nagg, lives in an ashbin, also having lost her legs in the bicycling accident years ago. She dies in the play to the great distress of Nagg.

Themes

Live or Die?

The characters, trapped in their single room occupy themselves with routines and tasks. Hamm is paralyzed and blind, Nagg and Nell cannot leave their ashbins, and the action of the play occurs in a single room, outside of which life evidently cannot survive. These characters struggle to move on or take action, and the actions they do take are often stagnant and nondescript. Each is dependent upon another for his or her very survival and Hamm questions the benefit of continuing life at all, often pestering nag for the ultimate painkiller—death.

The existence of God is also questioned and indirectly denied, painting a bleak picture of life as hard and without redemption, directed by the needs of handicapped tyrants like Hamm. When Hamm orders both Clov and Nagg to pray to God, Hamm cries in agony, "The bastard! He doesn't exist!" Hamm and the other characters, in their stagnant misery and frustrations, lack faith in a benevolent promise of God to reprieve or redeem their anguish. Life seems a merciless cycle of desire and grief, of handicaps and ashbins, and, to these characters, death is no reward for enduring that cycle. The characters of *Endgame* maneuver through lives of emotional strife that anticipate death, though they lack the means to achieve it on their own.

Interdependence

One of the most obvious themes of *Endgame* is the necessity of interdependence, even if the relationship is one of hate. Clov, for example, depends on Hamm for food since Hamm is the only one who knows the combination to the cupboard. Hamm relies completely on Clov for movement and vision. Critics often compare *Endgame* to Beckett's previous drama *Waiting for Godot*, noting that characters in both plays are grouped in pairs. *Endgame* is bleaker and more perplexing because it lacks the hope for redemption that *Waiting for Godot* contains.

Generational Conflict

Generational conflict, particularly between father and son, also emerges as a prominent theme. Hamm twice tells a story about a father and son and seems to view parent-child relationships only in terms of power and resentment. Critics have argued that Hamm resents Nagg, his father, for not being kind to him when he was young, whereas Hamm resents Clov, his son, for being young at a time when his own life is in decline. *Endgame* has also been interpreted as a depiction of humanity's denial of such life processes as death and procreation.

Media Adaptations

- Released by Ambrose Video on DVD in 2002, the *Beckett on Film* DVD set is the first ever cinematic screening of all nineteen of Samuel Beckett's plays. The acclaimed *Beckett on Film* project brings together some of the most distinguished directors and actors working today. Directors include Atom Egoyan, Damien Hirst, Neil Jordan, Conor McPherson, Damien O'Donnell, David Mamet, Anthony Minghella, Karel Reisz, and Patricia Rozema. The exceptional acting talent involved includes Michael Gambon, the late Sir John Gielgud, John Hurt, Jeremy Irons, Julianne Moore, Harold Pinter, Alan Rickman, and Kristen Scott-

Thomas. Several of the films from the Beckett on Film project have been exhibited at international film festivals around the world including New York, Toronto, and Venice.

Artistry

Endgame is a self-reflexive work in which the hand of Beckett can often be seen. For example, Hamm's narration is at once taking its own course in developing his personality while it also comments on the idea of creation, alluding to the creative process of an author. At the end of the story Hamm talks about the difficulty of creation:

CLOV: Will it end soon?

HAMM: I'm afraid it will.

CLOV: Pah! You'll make up another.

HAMM: I don't know. (Pause.) I feel rather drained. The prolonged creative effort.

The characters make numerous, explicit references throughout *Endgame* to their roles as characters in a play. Hamm at one-point states: "I'm warming up for my last soliloquy." Clov, at another instance, announces: "This is what we call making an exit." Such self-reflexive references to the action of the play are representative of modernism and also suggest humankind's inclination for dramatization to assign meaning in life and help understand the world.

Humor

"Nothing is funnier than unhappiness." Though *Endgame* is dark, there is humor in the play. Clov's confusion over which items to fetch first and his antics with the ladder could be directly out of a film starring Charlie Chaplin, whom Beckett admired. Commenting on *Endgame* himself, Beckett identified the phrase "nothing is funnier than unhappiness" as key to the play's interpretation and performance.

Style

Words and Stage Directions

Endgame's visual performance and self-reflexive dialogue constantly remind the audience that they are watching a performance by actors. Hamm broods: "All kinds of fantasies! That I'm being watched!" This tells the audience that they are part of the structure of the play, just as words, physical movement, lighting, whistles, dogs, ladders, windows, and silence play their roles. Beckett uses stage directions to create dynamic relationships between characters and the things they require to live: Hamm needs his armchair, and Nagg and Nell require their ashbins. Beckett creates a vivid physical world to complement the powerful and stripped-down dialogue.

Beckett presents the characters' inability to understand through abstract language and stagnant dramatic structure. Beckett has stripped down and broken apart his words and sentences. Words are able to contradict each other and are often elliptic. Clov utters the first line of the play: "Finished, it's finished, nearly finished, it must be nearly finished." By beginning the play with the word "Finished," Beckett directs our attention toward endings. As Beckett's characters search themselves and the world around them, language reflects the precarious balance between understanding and confusion.

Topics for Further Study

- Beckett is often considered a forerunner to the absurdist movement in theater. Read Harold Pinter's *The Dumb Waiter* and David Mamet's *Glengarry, Glen Ross,* and write an essay on how you think their writing has been influenced by Samuel Beckett.

- Nagg and Nell, Hamm's parents, are in ashbins throughout the play. What comment does this make on society and our ideas and treatment of the elderly?

- Beckett's plays are filled with rituals. What rituals does Clov perform for Hamm, and what does this say about the master-servant relationship they are in?

- *Endgame* contains several elements of comedy. How do you feel these elements work in regard to the overall tone of the play? Why does Beckett make use of comedy in this manner? What is Beckett saying about life and the nature of comedy?

Beckett's Minor Plot

Samuel Beckett's plots are notable for their lack of the classical dramatic structure. The minor plot line of *Endgame* is that of Hamm's parents, Nagg and Nell. It is clear that they had a romantic love in their youth, but they now live in ashbins and are not well-taken-care-of by their son. The end of the play finds both Nagg and Nell dead, without having experienced much satisfaction throughout the play. Indeed, most of their interactions are attempts to recall their past happiness or to endure their current helpless situation.

Theater of the Absurd

Drama known as the theater of the absurd begins in the 1950s. *Endgame*, Beckett's first play after *Waiting for Godot*, continues in the tradition that *Waiting for Godot* established.

Historical Context

Nuclear Capability

Although Beckett does not place the characters and actions of *Endgame* in a specific time and place, the play's only set can be viewed as a bomb shelter after a nuclear bomb has detonated and destroyed much, if not all, life outside the shelter. This was certainly a looming fear when Beckett wrote the play and when it was performed in 1957. Although today this fear is still present, in 1957 the fear was at an all-time high, and the likelihood of such an event seemed all too possible and near.

The Cold War

The late 1950s and the 1960s were dominated by the cold war, an intense rivalry between the United States and its allies against the Soviet Union. After World War II, Europe was divided into two zones of power, a capitalist west and a socialist east. The rivalry soon became worldwide, and there was always a threat that it could have developed into full-scale nuclear war. The struggle did become violent in 1950 when communist North Korea invaded South Korea, beginning the Korean War, which ended with the country divided.

The Eisenhower Doctrine

The Eisenhower Doctrine, announced by United States President Dwight D. Eisenhower on January 5, 1957, pledged military and economic support to any Middle Eastern country needing help in resisting communist aggression. Marking another escalation in the cold war, the doctrine was intended to check the increase of Soviet influence in the Middle East and the increasingly strong Soviet support given the Arab states.

The Absurdists

Of the French writers known as the absurdists, Arthur Adamov, Eugène Ionesco, Jean Genet, and Samuel Beckett were the most significant. In the late 1930s and early 1940s, writers were trying to overthrow dramatic conventions and wanted to challenge audiences with something new. Antonin Artaud wrote *The Theatre and Its Double* (1938), which advocated a "theatre of cruelty," and in 1943 Jean-Paul Sartre wrote *Being and Nothingness* and *No Exit,* which dramatize Sartre's existentialist viewpoint. Sartre's viewpoint, combined with Albert Camus's writings, provided the building blocks for the absurdist movement, which began to take shape in the early 1950s.

In 1952, Ionesco premiered his play *The Chairs,* which is an excellent example of the theater of the absurd. However, it was not until 1953 and the premiere of *En Attendant Godot*, or *Waiting for Godot*, that absurdism reached a popular and international audience.

Waiting for Godot is perhaps the best-known work from the absurdist movement. The two-act tragicomedy tells the story of two old men, Vladimir and Estragon, who cannot decide if they should leave or stay and wait for Godot, who may or may not arrive and rescue them from their desperate situation. *Endgame* takes this struggle to the next level as Hamm and Clov struggle with the meaning, if there is any, of living at all. Beckett's importance to the absurdist movement is obvious, but saying that he is an absurdist writer is not giving full credit to his wide range of work. Beckett's writing stands out above the other absurdist works in its ingenuity, universality, and humanity.

Critical Overview

When *Endgame* opened in 1957, Beckett described the event as "rather grim, like playing to mahogany, or rather teak." Indeed, most critics found the play bewildering or they disliked it. Kenneth Tynan in the *Observer* said that Beckett's new play made it "clear that his purpose is neither to move nor to help us. For him, man is a pygmy who connives at his own inevitable degradation." Marc Bernard in *Nouvelles litteraires* said that he constantly had the impression that he was listening to a medieval fantasy or comic poem in which allegorical characters, fake scholasticism, and Aristotelian reasoning were made into a mixture in which metaphysics suddenly took on a farcical tone. He considered Hamm "the intellectual, paralysed, blind as talkative as a fourteenth century doctor. He is waited upon by the Common Man, half way between man and beast" who "has been given a simian appearance: long, dangling arms, curved spine. The intellectual's father and mother are stuffed into two dustbins; from time to time a lid is lifted and one of the parents begins to talk." T. C. Worsley in the *Listener* said of *Waiting for Godot*, "Mr. Beckett's neurosis and mine were for quite long stretches on the same theme; in *Endgame* they never tangled. He has, in *Endgame*, ... expanded not the public but the private images. He has concentrated not on what is common between his audiences and him but on what is private in himself."

When *Endgame* was produced on Broadway in 1980, directed by Jopseh Chaikin and starring Daniel Setzer as Hamm and Michael Gross as Clov, it had become considered a classic. Mel Gussow, wrote in the *New York Times* that "Mr. Chaikin and Mr. Setzer never forget the play's portent, but neither do they shortchange its mordant humor. The director approaches *Endgame* as a gem to be played, as a piece to be performed. Mr. Chaikin is an experimental artist who is scrupulous when dealing with classics." He concludes, "the play is profound. The acting is prodigious."

Compare & Contrast

- **1950s:** The United States and the Soviet Union are split over Middle East loyalties and support. Fear of a nuclear war increases.

    Today: The United States and England engage in war with Iraq. The United States wages war on terrorism throughout the world. North Korea possesses nuclear weapons, and the potential for nuclear war again seems all too possible.

- **1950s:** Russian scientists launch Sputnik into orbit, initiating the space race between the United States and Russia.

Today: Beginning in the 1990s, Russian cosmonauts worked together with American astronauts on the space station Mir. The United States and Russia continue to have cooperative working efforts in space exploration and research.

- **1950s:** Eugene O'Neill is posthumously awarded the Pulitzer Prize in drama for *Long Day's Journey into Night.*
  Today: *Topdog/Underdog* by Suzan-Lori Parks wins the Pulitzer Prize for drama.

- **1950s:** Albert Camus receives the Nobel Prize for literature "for his important literary production, which with clear-sighted earnestness illuminates the problems of the human conscience in our times."
  Today: Imre Kertsz (Hungary) receives the Nobel Prize for literature "for writing that upholds the fragile experience of the individual against the barbaric arbitrariness of history."

What Do I Read Next?

- *Waiting for Godot* (1953) is Samuel Beckett's best-known play about two tramps waiting for the elusive Godot.

- *The Unnamable* (1953) is the third novel of Beckett's trilogy, including *Molloy* (1951) and *Malone Dies* (1951). All three novels, which were originally written in French, are interior monologues containing flashes of dark humor.

- *Krapp's Last Tape* (1958) is another of Beckett's stage plays. It consists of a monologue in which the aged Krapp attempts to recapture the intensity of days long passed by listening to recordings of his younger self.

- Eugène Ionseco's play *The Chairs* (1958) is about a man who had opportunities to lead a great life but led a simple life with his wife instead. After many years, he decides to tell society his secret. The only characters in the play are the old man, the woman, and the person the old man hires to tell the world his secret. This play is a staple work of the theater of the absurd.

- David Mamet's *Glengarry Glenn Ross* (1983) is an excellent example of the influence Beckett has had on the craft of writing plays. Mamet was highly influenced by Harold Pinter, to whom *Glengarry Glenn Ross* is dedicated, and Pinter was highly influenced by Beckett.

- Harold Pinter's *The Birthday Party* (1958) follows Stanley, an out-of-work pianist in a seaside boarding house. Stanley is mysteriously threatened and taken over by two intruders, who present him with a bizarre indictment of unexplained crimes.

- Anthony Cronin's *Samuel Beckett: The Last Modernist* (1997) is an ambitious and well-written biography of Samuel Beckett the writer, artist, and person.

Sources

Aristotle, "VI," in *Aristotle's Poetics,* translated by S. H. Butcher, Hill and Wang, 1989, p. 61.

Bernard, Marc, Review of *Endgame,* in *Nouvelles litteraires,* May 5, 1957.

Clarke, P. H., "Translator's Foreword," in *Chess Endings: Essential Knowledge,* by Y. Averbakh, Pergamon Press, 1966, p. vii.

Cronin, Anthony, "Chapter Twenty-Nine," in *Samuel Beckett: The Last Modernist,* HarperCollins, 1997, pp. 459–60.

Gussow, Mel, "The Stage: Chaikin Directs Beckett's *Endgame,*" in the *New York Times,* January 14, 1980.

Tynan, Kenneth, Review of *Endgame,* in the *Observer,* April 7, 1957.

Worsley, T. C., Review of *Endgame,* in the *Listener,* November 4, 1957.

Further Reading

Abbott, H. Porter, *The Fiction of Samuel Beckett: Form and Effect,* University of California Press, 1973.

> This book contains chapters on Beckett's early short fiction and the relationship between his stories and novels.

Bair, Deidre, *Samuel Beckett: A Biography,* Harcourt Brace Jovanovich, 1978.

> This biography about the reclusive Samuel Beckett is broad in scope and understandably flawed.

Ben-Zvi, Linda, *Samuel Beckett,* Twayne Publishers, 1986.

> Because of the large scope of Beckett's writings, this study of Beckett's complete works has necessitated a brief coverage of each work.

Bloom, Harold, ed., *Samuel Beckett's "Endgame,"* Modern Critical Interpretations series, Chelsea House Publishers, 1988.

> Bloom brings together a representative selection of what many consider to be the best eight critical interpretations of the play.

Coe, Richard, *Samuel Beckett,* Grove Press, 1964.

> Coe's study of Beckett focuses on his philosophical background.

Cohn, Ruby, *Back to Beckett,* Princeton University Press, 1973.

> Cohn presents a detailed study of Beckett's fiction and drama.

Zurbrugg, Nicholas, "*Ill Seen Ill Said* and the Sense of an Ending," in *Beckett's Later Fiction and Drama: Texts for Company,* edited by James Acheson and Kateryna Arthur, Macmillan Press, 1987.

> Zurbrugg asserts that *Ill Seen Ill Said* is not so much a story as a poetic evocation of those rituals by which the living and the dead within Beckett's fiction endlessly, and quite ineffectively, strive to attain a definitive "sense of an ending."

Lightning Source UK Ltd.
Milton Keynes UK
UKHW021256150722
405908UK00010B/1914